D1410611

A DORLING KINDERSLEY BOOK

Project Editor Mary Atkinson
Art Editor Ivan Finnegan
Design Assistant Chris Drew
Deputy Managing Editor Dawn Sirett
Deputy Managing Art Editor
C. David Gillingwater
Production Josie Alabaster
Picture Research Joanne Beardwell
Photography Peter Anderson,
Dave King, and Gary Lewis
Illustrator Ellis Nadler

First published in Great Britain in 1997
by Dorling Kindersley Limited,
9 Henrietta Street, London WC2E 8PS

Copyright © 1997 Dorling Kindersley Limited, London
Visit us on the World Wide Web at http://www.dk.com

All rights reserved. No part of this publication may be
reproduced, stored in a retrieval system, or transmitted
in any form or by any means, electronic, mechanical,
photocopying, recording or otherwise, without the prior
written permission of the copyright owner.

A CIP catalogue record for this book
is available from the British Library.

ISBN 0-7513-5509-7

Colour reproduction by Chromagraphics, Singapore
Printed and bound in Italy by L.E.G.O.

Dorling Kindersley would like to thank the following
for their kind permission to reproduce photographs:
t=top, b=bottom, c=centre, l=left, r=right

Bruce Coleman / C.B. & D.W. Frith 14-15c;
Frank Lane Picture Agency / Mark Newman 19br;
NHPA / Rich Kirchner 14bl; **Oxford Scientific Films** /
Animals Animals / Hans & Judy Beste 10bl, / Konrad Wothe
19tl; **Planet Earth Pictures** / Gary Bell 4cr, 8bl, 10-11c, /
Peter J. Oxford 9br.

Scale
Look out for drawings
like this – they show
the size of the animals
compared with people.

Babirusa
Page 12

Marabou stork
Page 17

Crested porcupine
Page 20

Tasmanian devil
Page 10

Komodo
dragon
Page 8

WEIRD
CREATURES
OF THE WILD

Written by Theresa Greenaway

Ground hornbill
Page 16

Tapir
Page 6

Cassowary
Page 14

Echidna
Page 21

Guanaco
Page 18

DORLING KINDERSLEY
LONDON • NEW YORK • STUTTGART • MOSCOW

Tapir

The strange-looking tapir lives in swampy rainforests. Its hefty body and short, strong legs are just the right shape to push through thick undergrowth.

🐾 The tapir's trunk is really an extra-long nose and top lip.

🐾 Tapirs leave piles of droppings as they move around to mark their territory.

🐾 A tapir can hide underwater. It uses its trunk just like a snorkel, poking it out to breathe.

Funny feet
Tapirs have unusual feet. They have four toes on each front foot, but only three on each hind foot.

Hoofed animals, such as tapirs, walk on their toes. A hoof is a large toenail that protects the toe bone.

🐾 An animal's **territory** is an area of land that it defends from others. 🐾

The Brazilian tapir's short, stiff mane helps to protect its neck from overhanging branches.

The tapir has poor eyesight, but a good sense of smell. Nostrils at the tip of its trunk allow it to sniff out the tastiest roots and ripest shoots.

Scale

Camouflage colours
The Malayan tapir's beautiful black-and-white markings break up its outline so it can hide among the dark shadows of jungle trees.

Tapirs need their strong legs to escape predators such as hungry crocodiles or jaguars.

Predators are animals that hunt other animals for food.

Komodo dragon

🐾 A Komodo dragon can reach 3 metres in length. That's one and a half times as long as your bed.

🐾 When a Komodo dragon wants to keep another dragon away, it uses its long, powerful tail like a sword.

🐾 Komodo dragons group together to share large catches. However, the biggest lizards seize all the best pieces.

Komodo dragons are the world's largest lizards. They are found only on Indonesian islands, where they feed on goats, pigs, and deer – dead or alive! Sometimes they'll also attack unwary tourists.

Suitable suit
The Komodo dragon is covered in scales, which protect it from sunburn and from becoming dehydrated.

This Komodo dragon lives in a zoo. A special red lotion has been applied to its skin to keep it healthy.

Each toe on this giant lizard's feet ends in a long, sharp claw.

🐾 A **dehydrated** animal doesn't have enough water in its body to stay healthy. 🐾

The Komodo dragon has ear openings on the sides of its head. It relies both on hearing and on sight to catch prey.

Cold-blooded hunter
Like all reptiles, Komodo dragons are cold-blooded. They need the sun's warmth for energy, but must not get too hot, so they hunt early in the day.

Scale

The Komodo dragon's tail is about the same length as the rest of its body.

Fast movers
Komodo dragons use their strong legs to chase prey. They can run fast over short distances, swim, and even climb low trees.

Cold-blooded animals depend on their surroundings for warmth.

9

Tasmanian devil

These fierce-looking creatures scavenge and hunt on the Australian island of Tasmania. They are called devils because of their spine-chilling screams.

This large, broad head supports very powerful jaw muscles.

Sharp, pointed teeth are for tearing meat.

Creatures of the night
At dusk, Tasmanian devils leave their daytime nests in hollow logs or rocky clefts to begin hunting.

Long whiskers help the Tasmanian devil to feel its way when it's hunting at night.

Scale

When an animal searches for dead animals to eat, it is **scavenging**.

With their stocky bodies, these animals are suited mainly for scavenging or hunting slow prey.

Finger food

The Tasmanian devil is one of the few predators that uses its paws to push food into its mouth.

Thick fur keeps the Tasmanian devil warm even on cold winter nights.

AMARING FACTS

🐾 A Tasmanian devil's strong jaws can crunch through the bones larger predators leave behind.

🐾 The Tasmanian devil has a huge appetite. It will eat everything from farmyard chickens to poisonous snakes.

The Tasmanian devil's short legs are ideal for foraging in dense undergrowth.

🐾 Like the kangaroo, the Tasmanian devil is a marsupial. A baby Tasmanian devil lives inside its mother's pouch until it is about fifteen weeks old.

🐾 A **marsupial** is an animal that is carried in its mother's pouch as a baby. 🐾

Babirusa

The babirusa is a type of wild pig from Indonesia. It lives in small family groups. A male babirusa has four incredible, curling tusks that keep growing until they almost touch his eyes.

A babirusa's nose is always moist to help it pick up scent.

Pigging out
Babirusas eat mostly plants, especially fallen fruit. They have powerful teeth for crunching seeds and nuts.

Each foot has four toes, but the outer two only touch the ground when the babirusa walks on uneven, swampy ground.

Tusks are long teeth that can be seen even when an animal shuts its mouth.

Thick, protective skin hangs in folds and creases.

Brown-grey skin colour matches the mud in which babirusas often wallow, helping them to hide.

The tusks on most pigs poke out of their mouths. But, a male babirusa's two curly, upper tusks actually grow right through the skin on the top of his snout.

Scale

A fast getaway
The babirusa's long legs help it to run quickly to escape predators such as tigers.

Males use their large curving tusks to show off to each other – and to attract female babirusas.

Unlike most other pigs, which have bodies covered in stiff bristles, the babirusa is almost completely hairless.

To **wallow** in mud is to roll about in it.

13

Cassowary

A cassowary has a tall, bony casque on top of its head.

The cassowary may look comical, but it is actually one of the deadliest animals in Papua New Guinea. One kick from this bad-tempered bird can kill a person.

Both males and females have red, fleshy throat wattles.

Scale

The female lays up to eight eggs in a nest on the forest floor. The male then guards the eggs and keeps them warm.

A lonely life
Cassowaries are solitary birds, each one guarding its own territory. Males and females meet only to breed.

A **casque** is a horn-like bump that grows on top of a bird's beak and head.

Only adult cassowaries have these glossy black feathers. The young birds have brown feathers for camouflage.

No-one is quite sure why a cassowary has a casque on top of its head, but it may be a "crash helmet" for charging through dense bush.

During courtship, the bright blue skin on a male cassowary's neck swells up and quivers.

A cassowary can be up to 1.8 metres tall. That's about the same height as a tall adult.

Thick skin protects a cassowary's legs from getting cut as it runs through tough undergrowth.

When threatened, a cassowary charges at its attacker, slashing out with its long, sharp claws on each inside toe.

What big feet
The cassowary needs its wide-toed feet and strong legs to support its big, heavy body.

Courtship is when a male or female animal tries to attract a mate. 15

Ground hornbill

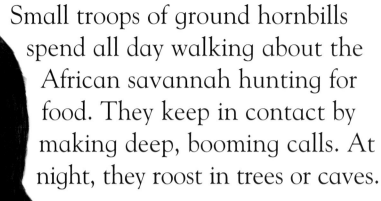

Small troops of ground hornbills spend all day walking about the African savannah hunting for food. They keep in contact by making deep, booming calls. At night, they roost in trees or caves.

Both young and female Abyssinian ground hornbills have blue skin on their throats, while the adult males have pink skin.

A hornbill flies with slow, powerful beats of its large wings.

Scale

AMAZING FACTS

 When hunting food, ground hornbills may walk up to 19 km a day.

 Birds' casques and beaks are made of a similar material to your fingernails.

From scratch
Ground hornbills find insects to eat by scratching at the ground with their sharp claws.

When on the ground, the hornbill uses its tail to help it balance.

When a bird **roosts,** it settles somewhere to sleep or rest.

Marabou stork

Using their long, pointed beaks like pickaxes, marabou storks clean up the remains of all kinds of African animals. These incredibly tall, fearless birds can scare even the vultures away from a carcass.

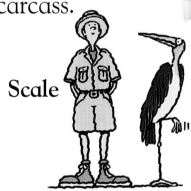

Scale

AMAZING FACTS

From head to toe, a marabou stork can measure 1.5 metres. That's about as high as the roof of a car.

Spread out, a marabou's wings can span up to 4 metres – wider than two adult people lying head-to-toe.

Clean-cut bird
Even after a messy meal, these storks' bald heads are easy to keep clean.

Long legs help this stork to stride through marshland.

Strong toes grip the branches of its night roost.

Guanaco

These hardy South American animals roam wild on the high slopes of the Andes mountains. Each small herd is guarded by a male, who bleats a loud alarm to warn of danger.

Scale

A narrow muzzle and a split upper lip allow the guanaco to nibble very short grass.

Mountain meals
Guanacos are herbivores. They graze on mountain grasses and wild plants.

A **herbivore** is an animal that eats mainly plants.

Bachelor group

When young males in the herd become adults, the older male leader chases them away. The young males then join up in groups.

🐾 On high mountains, there is less oxygen in the air. But guanacos cope better than we do. Their blood is especially good at taking in oxygen.

🐾 Guanacos raise and lower their short tails to send each other messages.

🐾 Some guanacos live up to 4,500 metres above sea-level. At this height, few trees are able to survive, only thick, tough mountain grasses.

Cold-weather wear

Nights can be bitterly cold on the windy mountainsides. Guanacos need their thick, woolly coats to keep warm.

Like its relative, the camel, the guanaco only has two toes on each foot.

🐾 **Oxygen** is a gas in the air that living things need in order to live. 🐾

Crested porcupine

When frightened, the African porcupine rattles its quills and stamps its feet. If this doesn't scare away a predator, the porcupine rushes backwards, jabbing its long, sharp quills into its enemy.

Scale

A porcupine raises its quills to make itself look bigger when threatened.

Soft spot
A baby porcupine suckles milk near its mother's front legs – where it's not too prickly.

There are no quills on the face, just stiff bristles.

A porcupine's long, hollow spines are called **quills**.

AMATING FACT

A porcupine's quills can be up to 35 cm long. That's about three times as long as one of your hands.

Hollow, lightweight quills are not too heavy to carry around.

This Australian marsupial is one of only three mammals to lay eggs. After the eggs hatch, the babies crawl into their mother's pouch. They stay there for up to ten weeks, growing bigger and stronger.

Scale

Nosy creature
The echidna uses its long snout to poke deep into crevices, sniffing out tasty ants and termites.

Short, sharp spines protect the echidna from predators, such as dogs.

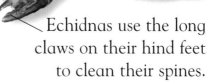

Echidnas use the long claws on their hind feet to clean their spines.

The echidna's spines stick out through a layer of bristly hair.

 Mammals are animals that suckle milk from their mothers when they are young. 21